HEALING
THE THERAP

Steve Daily, MS, LP

WOODNEATH
PRESS

Ashley,

I hope you enjoy my book of poetry.

Steve

Published by Woodneath Press
8900 NE Flintlock Rd.
Kansas City, MO 64157

Please visit FeelGoodEnough.com for downloadable PDF versions of the poems and accompanying journal exercises.

Publisher's Cataloguing-in-Publication
(Provided by Woodneath Press: A Program of Mid-Continent Public Library)

Daily, Steve
    Healing the Heart and Mind: The Therapist's Workbook of Poetry
    p. cm.
ISBN-13: 978-1-942337-11-9

    I. Self-help / General
    II. Poetry / Subjects & Themes / Inspirational & Religious
    III. Body, Mind & Spirit / Mindfulness & Meditation

DEDICATION

I would like to dedicate this poetry workbook to the clients I have seen over the years who have taught me so much. Without them this work of art would have never been created.

TABLE OF CONTENTS

INTRODUCTION   i

PERSONAL GROWTH   1
    Who Am I?   3
    Forgiving   6
    Courage to be Human   10
    Too Often I Chose Fear   13
    Getting Unstuck   16

MANAGING EMOTIONS   23
    Anger   25
    Depression is Often Misunderstood   28
    Coping with Panic   31
    Taming Emotions   34
    Letting Go of Guilt and Shame   38

RECOVERING FROM PAINFUL EXPERIENCES   43
    Going on After Trauma   45
    Letting Go   49
    Choose Life   52
    Change is a Part of Life   57
    On Angel's Wings   60

INTERPERSONAL HEALTH   65
    Bobbers and Sinkers   67
    Listening is a Gift of Love   70
    Encourage Me   73
    Humor is Good Medicine   76
    Pleasing can be Costly   79

FINDING HAPPINESS   83
    Happiness   85
    Children are Precious Gifts   89
    Smiles have Healing Power   92
    Master of My Mind   95
    Gratitude is a Precious Gift   98

DIALECTICAL BEHAVIOR THERAPY 103
    What is Mindfulness? 105
    What is Interpersonal Effectiveness? 108
    What is Emotional Regulation? 111
    What is Distress Tolerance? 114
    What is Radical Acceptance? 117

SPIRITUAL POEMS 121
    Allowing Another to Care 123
    The Healer of Broken Hearts 126
    Thank You for Today 130
    Lord, Help Me Forgive 133
    The Path of Grace 136

NOTE TO DBT THERAPISTS 141
REFERENCES 142
ABOUT THE AUTHOR 143

Do you believe poetry can help heal the mind and heart? I do. I have written this little workbook to help persons reading it experience personal growth and emotional healing. I have worked most of my adult life as a psychologist and therapist and have frequently shared poetry with clients to help them through difficult times.

As a therapist, I help clients clarify changes they wish to make in their life, support them, and provide them with strategies and skills to make those changes. Poetry can help clients remember an important truth they just learned. It can move clients emotionally so they can feel something and go beyond mere rational thought. Poetry can assist struggling persons to become aware of unhealthy beliefs that keep them stuck and prevent them from experiencing more happiness and peace of mind.

This workbook can increase awareness of how being around negative persons can bring you down, while being around positive and encouraging persons can lift your spirits. It contains poems to help you deal with grief after losing someone near to your heart. It provides helpful ideas for understanding depression, coping with panic, and going on after experiencing a traumatic event.

In this little workbook, you will encounter ideas to help you tame intense emotions and understand the importance of letting go of those things outside your control. You will realize the power of gratitude and the benefits of having a forgiving heart. The power of encouraging others and being a good listener will also be revealed. In total there are 35 poems that cover an array of topics related to growth and emotional healing.

I hope you, as a reader, will find my writings to speak to you in a way that promotes your personal growth. All of my poems have been written to encourage healing of hearts and minds. We often suffer due to being caught up in a pattern of negative thinking and behavior. If we do not see the error of our ways, we will continue down the same unproductive path.

Some of my poetry is spiritual in nature. As a therapist I am careful to respect my clients whether they believe there is no God, are agnostic, or practice a faith that is the same as or different than my own. My last five poems are ones that are more spiritual in nature and refer to a loving God. Many of my clients are Christian, and I will at times share some of my poems that are Christian in nature. I often talk briefly with my clients about their spiritual beliefs, so I will be able to best serve them.

Please feel free to share my poems with anyone. I hope that they can encourage others and promote positive change.

HOW TO USE THIS WORKBOOK

Here is how I have decided to organize this workbook. In each section I will first share a poem. Second, I will put forth five questions related to the poem to hopefully provoke thought. Third, I will share my reflections as the author of the poem. Finally, I will encourage you to write your response to three prompts in the JOURNAL TO GROW AND HEAL portion of the workbook.

In using this workbook, some readers may choose to simply read the poetry. Others will complete the workbook taking one poem at a time and completing the other three parts to deepen their understanding. Some will read the poems and then only complete the workbook portion for poems that personally concern them. Please use this workbook in a way that best meets your needs.

If you are a therapist, I would encourage you to at times give your client a copy of a specific poem that speaks to an issue with which they are struggling. For instance, the "Bobbers and Sinkers" poem could be used with clients needing to distance themselves from highly critical people and instead find more positive people to be around. Poems may also be used to reinforce a virtue that a client already possesses. Many find poetry to evoke deeper thought and to stir the heart. You may want to have your client complete the JOURNAL TO GROW AND HEAL portion of the workbook as a therapy assignment. Please visit FeelGoodEnough.com for downloadable PDF versions of the poems and accompanying journal exercises.

The poems are organized into categories. Poems 26 to 30 focus on five major topics related to Dialectical Behavior Therapy (DBT). Poems 31 to 35 are spiritual in nature and refer to God.

I hope you will find this workbook causes you to stop and reflect on your life. It is my intent that you as a reader will grow in some way as you read the poetry and do related journaling. Use this workbook as a gift to make positive changes in your life, and to share its truths with friends and family.

Personal Growth

The five poems in this section relate to the topic of personal growth. It is hoped that studying these poems will help you grow in different ways. Discovering who you are, learning to let go of vindictive emotions, developing the courage to be imperfect, taking positive risks, and learning ways to get unstuck are covered.

~ *Who Am I?* ~

Many go through life struggling to discover
who they are.
Some are burdened with feelings of unceasing
emptiness and worthlessness.
Others seem to feel good only in relation to
what others say to them.
So often we base our self-worth and self-image
on things external.
This leaves us quite vulnerable to being used
and manipulated by others.
I have come to realize that I am at my core,
my consciousness.
Each day I choose over and over what I will
think, feel and do.
It is in making the choice to believe and hope
that I define myself.
We each are only in part a product of our
experience and environment.
More importantly, we are what we value,
work for and do.
I choose to open my mind to new possibilities
for meaningful living.
Also I choose to give support and receive
help as needed.
In faith I choose to see light as each
new day dawns.
I am happy to be me and I hope you
are happy to be you.

QUESTIONS TO PONDER

1. Do you feel good about your self-image and believe you have worth?

2. Do you have a stable self-image or does your self-worth rise and fall quickly in response to others?

3. Do you believe you are a victim of your past, or do you believe your choices determine your life?

4. What do you deeply value in your life?

5. How could you change your self-image to allow you to experience more happiness?

REFLECTIONS OF THE AUTHOR

I work with many clients who experience unceasing feelings of emptiness and worthlessness. Childhood abuse often triggers a chain of thinking and feeling that becomes self-perpetuating. As a therapist, I find it quite challenging to help clients change their negative self-image.

There is no medication or quick fix for a damaged self-concept, and often a broken self-image must change before a person can really begin to experience peace of mind and more happiness. In my poem I point out that persons are more vulnerable to be manipulated when they base their self-worth on how others treat them.

I encourage readers of this poem to give some thought to how they see themselves. I also urge them to open their mind to new possibilities and to embrace a hopeful outlook. If you do not currently feel happy about who you are, I hope you will do what is needed to get there.

1. Write about some of your personal strengths and/or what you most like about yourself.

_____

_____

_____

2. Identify and journal about one personal weakness that you would like to change.

_____

_____

_____

3. Write briefly about the person you would ideally like to be.

_____

_____

_____

§

~ *Forgiving* ~

Forgiving is a choice I make to heal
emotional pain,
And it is not an invitation for others
to take advantage of me.

As long as I choose to fill my mind with
thoughts of vindictiveness,
I have given you control of my mind
and heart.

I forgive you because I no longer want
to give you a place in my heart,
For I want to have ample space to
experience joy and love.

I forgive you because I choose to enjoy
peace of mind,
And I cannot do so as long as I entertain
thoughts of getting even.

Often the actual wrongful action of
another is momentary,
But the holding onto can last for eternity
if we allow it.

I wish you well and hope that you will
grow to be a healthier person,
And in my forgiving you I choose to live
in the present and not the past.

I can choose nothing other than to
forgive you,
For I care too much for myself to
not let go.

QUESTIONS TO PONDER

1. Think about someone who hurt you or wronged you deeply. How do you feel about that person?

2. Do you currently want to get even with that person, or have you wanted to do so in the past?

3. What effect has the emotional injury had on your life?

4. Do you want to release or let go of those painful feelings?

5. What steps do you need to take to let go of those negative emotions so you are free to experience joy and peace of mind?

REFLECTIONS OF THE AUTHOR

I can remember being very envious of another person in high school. After hearing a sermon on forgiveness, the following day I remember forgiving that person in my mind and heart while I studied in the college library. Tears trickled down my cheeks, and it felt good to release those feelings of anger and envy.

For some clients forgiving can be a most difficult task which eludes them. In my poem on forgiving, I attempt to convey that forgiving is something one does for oneself. To choose not to forgive, keeps us trapped in negative feelings and ruminating thoughts.

As a therapist, I believe that forgiving involves several mental steps. One is to honestly recognize how we feel, and to clearly understand our beliefs that maintain those emotions. It is helpful to understand why the other person may have done what we find so hurtful. We need to look at how we may have contributed to the problem. We need to choose to forgive for our benefit. Forgiveness does not excuse the behavior, nor do we need to allow the person to continue to abuse us in any way.

1. Write about how someone hurt you deeply. What did they do and how did you feel?

_____

_____

_____

2. Write about what you have done that has fueled your negative feelings.

_____

_____

_____

3. Write down specific steps you might take to forgive the person and experience peace of mind.

_____

_____

_____

§

9

~ *Courage to be Human* ~

During the journey of life there are many fears
to be faced,
Including the fear of harm or death to oneself
or one's family.
Possibly one of the most important fears for
any to confront
Is the fear of imperfection — the fear of making
errors or mistakes.
Many of us have been taught that there is
no room for error,
And we often go through life pretending
we are perfect.
The costs persons pay for perfectionism are
excessive anxiety
And loneliness — for no one feels comfortable
around someone perfect.
There is much more peace of mind for one
who admits to imperfection —
For life becomes less fearful when you are
free to be human.
In admitting to doing something wrong, others
feel more at ease,
For they too can relate to silly mistakes made
along the way.
It is somewhat ironic that in being vulnerable
we become strong,
And in admitting our imperfection we become
less imperfect.

1. Do you have difficulty admitting mistakes?

2. Do you know someone who is a perfectionist? How do you feel around that person?

3. Do you agree that perfectionism contributes to anxiety and loneliness?

4. What are the benefits of developing the courage to be imperfect?

5. What steps have you taken to be human?

REFLECTIONS OF THE AUTHOR

The "Courage to be Human" poem was written to help individuals understand some of the difficulties that are related to perfectionism. For some persons, perfectionism triggers excessive anxiety and can cause interpersonal problems. I often explain to clients that some perfectionism can be beneficial, but excessive perfectionism can be harmful to one's mental health.

If you have a moderate amount of perfectionism, you are likely to take pride in cleaning your car or in painting a room. When you have done a good job, you will feel good. Others may admire and even compliment you on how well you do your task. If you have too much perfectionism, you will spend an excessive amount of time completing your task. You will look at it, and you will be self-critical. The slightest flaw will stand out to you. If others give you a genuine compliment, you will discount it because in your eyes you failed to do your best.

The poem points out the advantages of having the courage to be imperfect — the courage to be human. People who admit their mistakes help those around them to be comfortable. They also are less likely to be judgmental of others because they have learned to be more accepting of themselves and others. I hope you will take this poem to heart and will strive to develop the courage to be imperfect.

1. Write about a time you were being a perfectionist. How did you act and feel?

_____

_____

_____

_____

2. Have you learned to be human, or do you frequently find yourself wanting to appear perfect?

_____

_____

_____

3. What would be the benefits for you, if you were to strive to be human and admit when you mess up?

_____

_____

_____

_____

§

~ Too Often I Chose Fear ~

Each day in our life we have choices to make
where we pick either fear or love.
If we share our dreams publicly with others
we risk humiliation.
When we share our true feelings we risk
misunderstanding and ridicule.
To set worthy goals may bring demoralization
if we fail to reach them.

In my life I regret the many times I chose to
not risk and play it safe.
It is as though a little part of me died each
time I chose to listen to fear.
I avoided the anxiety and struggle that comes
with choosing love,
But I did not grow nor did I experience the
joy that comes from love.

You alone control the choices you make
traveling life's path.
My friend, I wish you well and hope you
have a wonderful journey.
I only caution you to make wise decisions
and to risk
Listening more to your heart than to
the voice of fear.

QUESTIONS TO PONDER

1. Can you think of something you regret not doing, because you listened to your fear?

2. How would your life be different if you were to overcome many of your irrational fears?

3. How did you feel when you chose love over fear?

4. What does the following line mean to you?
   "A little part of me died each time I chose to listen fear."

5. What do most people experience when they find the courage to face their fears?

REFLECTIONS OF THE AUTHOR

Jerry Jampolsky's book, *Love Is Letting Go of Fear*, has had a positive impact on my life. My poem reflects the key idea of his book, which is that we must choose to love or we retreat into fear. I believe fear is the emotion that most frequently hinders people's emotional growth and character development.

I often give this poem to clients who need to take positive risks, but their fear holds them back. Way too often we allow our irrational and catastrophic thinking to prevent us from taking those steps that would lead to meaningful living.

There have been numerous times in my life where good ideas and worthy goals have died due to either my irrational fear or my unwillingness to devote effort to a task. I believe we can be too driven and fail to smell the roses along the way. I also know that it is easy to fall into devoting our time to things that provide little fulfillment. I personally have watched way too much television.

I hope my poem will nudge you to choose love over fear.

1. Write about a time when you failed to take a risk and it caused you to regret your decision.

   _____

   _____

   _____

   _____

2. Write how you think your life might be different if you had the courage to take positive risks.

   _____

   _____

   _____

   _____

3. Write what the phrase "you have to choose between love and fear" means to you.

   _____

   _____

   _____

   _____

§

~ *Getting Unstuck* ~

Many go through life like a man
driving down a muddy road.
When his car gets stuck in the mud
he puts more pedal to the metal.
He continues to do more of the same
as his car digs deeper and deeper.
Then at lasts he shouts, "Why do these
things always happen to me?"

The rules to getting unstuck are simple
and yet difficult to realize.
Accept that life is hard and it will
become less difficult.
Focus on doing what is in your control
and let go of the rest.
Choose to have peace of mind instead of
trying to prove you're right.

Being a victim or the captain of your
ship is a choice,
A most important choice that will
bind or free you.
If you accept responsibility for owning
your problems,
Then and only then can you begin
to look for solutions.

In life things are always as they should be
for that is how they are.
If it is cloudy and rainy it makes no sense
to think it should be sunny.
For it is as it is and not as you may
wish it to be.
You can choose to accept life as it is
or be forever fighting it.

Have a grateful heart and be happy
for the gifts you have,
And realize that happiness flows
from your gift to love.
Learn that forgiveness frees us to
let go of bitterness,
And accept that wrongs often come
from human weakness.

Take joy in recognizing the goodness
within others,
And freely encourage with every
opportunity to do so.
Respond to compliments given by
saying thank you,
And believe the encouraging words
of others who care.

Let go of the need to sacrifice
for it leads to resentment,
But instead find joy in giving with
no anticipation of receiving.
Do not react defensively to verbal
attack from friend or foe,
And instead welcome it as a way
of understanding another's fear.

Be aware that the quest for
perfection is futile,
But one can strive to have a loving
and forgiving heart.
When what you're doing is not
at all working,
Then do something differently and
you will become unstuck.

QUESTIONS TO PONDER

1. Do you keeping making the same mistakes over and over?

2. Do you get caught up continually thinking that life is unfair?

3. How can you let go of your negativity and find more peace of mind?

4. Do you own your problems and take responsibility for your life?

5. Have you learned to forgive and see all persons as having weaknesses just like you?

REFLECTIONS OF THE AUTHOR

I tend to give the "Getting Unstuck" poem to clients who are failing to make much progress in achieving their therapy goals. Everyone I know at times gets caught up repeating an ineffective pattern of behavior. In AA, insanity is defined as doing the same thing over and over and expecting different results.

This poem summarizes much that I have learned during years of doing therapy. Life at times can be hard and painful, and it feels worse when we think it's not fair. Our emotions are more influenced by how we react than by what happens to us. We begin finding solutions to our problems when we stop blaming others or ourselves. We find more joy in life when we focus on the goodness in others and realize our own.

I encourage you to accept life as it is. If you can take steps to make it better, please do. Don't get caught up in negative thinking that breeds feelings of helplessness. Remember the saying, "It's better to light one little candle than to curse the darkness."

1. Write about something you do that you would like to do less. What keeps you from changing?

_____

_____

_____

_____

2. Clearly visualize the way you would like to be. Write about how you would feel being that way.

_____

_____

_____

_____

3. Write about someone you need to forgive. How can you forgive without allowing future abuse?

_____

_____

_____

_____

§

20

MANAGING EMOTIONS

The poems in this part of the poetry workbook relate to the topic of understanding and managing emotions. The five poems discuss the potential harm of raging anger, help persons understand depression, provide ideas for coping with panic, explain how emotions can be tamed, and suggest a path for letting go of guilt and shame.

~ *Anger* ~

Anger is like a raging bull that destroys and maims,
A frightening beast when freed — one most untamed.
It is quite similar to a quickly burning wild fire
Carving a path of devastation — spreading ever so far.

Just as the air we breathe, anger is a part of life —
An unwelcomed companion or relative not liked.
And yet it should be noted that anger has its place
Of assisting us in setting boundaries and saving face.

It is not good to stuff our feelings of resentment and rage,
For it will eat at our gut and cause us to quickly age.
Anger buried deep within, like a splinter left, will fester
Spreading infection through the body — bringing disaster.

It is difficult to manage the anger we intensely feel,
But unless we try — the price we pay is all too real.
Loss of self-esteem, and much we truly value
Will be the cost of avoiding what we need to do.

To manage our anger we must first be willing to own
Complete responsibility for thoughts and vocal tone.
We always have a choice regardless of what others do,
To erupt in rage or to choose to do something new.

In time we can learn skills regarding how to express,
Our feelings assertively so conflict will be less.
It is a challenge to learn to use our anger constructively,
But the risk is worthwhile and I know this truly.

1. In what ways can anger at times be our friend?

2. Have you experienced the harm of erupting in anger and saying or doing things you regret?

3. Why is it not good to simply stuff your feelings?

4. Do you agree that to manage your anger you must take full responsibility for thoughts and words?

5. Is it worth investing time in learning to be less aggressive and defensive?

REFLECTIONS OF THE AUTHOR

I have counseled many persons having difficulty managing their anger over the years. I typically explain that anger is neither good or bad — it is simply an emotion. I discuss with my clients that our thoughts are what determines if we rage like a bull or speak with some wisdom and understanding.

In my poem on anger, I point out that uncontrolled anger can be quite destructive. Aggressive words and actions can cause persons to lose what they most value. The person who lives in a state of relentless rage pushes others away. Who wants to be abused and screamed at over and over?

The poem also shows us that we can gradually overcome our anger by honestly speaking up about our concerns, accepting full responsibility for our actions, and by learning to respond differently when we realize we are angry. I hope that my poem may give you some insight into anger and a few ideas on things you can do differently to tame your raging bull.

1. Write what you typically do when you experience anger. Do you tend to stuff it or blow up?

_____

_____

_____

2. Journal briefly about how anger has created some problems for you.

_____

_____

_____

3. Write about how you handle your anger better now or how you hope to handle it better in the future.

_____

_____

_____

_____

§

~ *Depression is Often Misunderstood* ~

Depression is a most painful disease,
and it is often misunderstood by so many.
When severe, it drains a person of all energy
leaving one for a time a living corpse.

It is not a state of mind that anyone wants,
and it does not simply go away at one's will.
Depression is a disease that disrupts sleep,
and robs so many of the desire to even eat.

In a depressed state, one has low self-esteem
with feelings of helplessness and no hope.
Hurtful memories tend to be magnified,
and joyful memories for a time are lost.

Decisions may be painfully difficult to make,
and interest in everyday activities vanish.
Many experience feelings of guilt and shame
based solely on irrational thought.

Deep depression often necessitates both
medical and psychological treatment.
Depressed persons most of all need
support and understanding of their illness.

It does no good and actually causes harm
to place blame on one for being depressed.
Someone to listen, care, and be present is
what one with depression desires and needs.

1. Do you know someone who suffers from severe depression?

2. Have you ever experienced deep depression?

3. What might you do to be more supportive and understanding of those with depression?

4. What do you believe a person can do to gradually improve their mood when they are depressed?

5. What is meant by this saying?
   "If you do what you feel like doing when you're depressed, you will become more depressed."

REFLECTIONS OF THE AUTHOR

I have written this poem on depression to validate how difficult it is for those who experience severe depression. Many of my clients who are deeply depressed find that family and friends are unable to really understand what they are going through. I hope my poem both validates them and helps others to realize that depression is real and quite difficult to manage.

I explain to my depressed clients that inactivity, procrastination, and isolation fuel depression. There are numerous things a person can do to begin to manage depression. Exercising, spending time with supportive people, improving sleep, healthy eating, and changing irrational beliefs all help to lessen depression. Persons who are severely depressed often benefit from anti-depressant medication.

If you are battling depression, please get help. If you have a friend or family member who is depressed, give them support and encourage them to get help.

1. Write about a time when you were depressed. What did you experience?

_____

_____

_____

_____

2. Journal briefly about how situational depression (job loss, death of a pet, etc.) differs from chronic depression.

_____

_____

_____

_____

3. Write about several things you might do to support someone you know who is depressed.

_____

_____

_____

_____

§

~ Coping with Panic ~

Out of nowhere at times there comes
intense fear,
That is overpowering and leaves me
feeling so defenseless.
My heart beats rapidly feeling like
it's about to explode,
And I find myself gasping for air as
I take quick breaths.
Thoughts of dying and going crazy
race through my mind,
As I fear looking foolish to others and
being embarrassed.
There is truly nothing to fear but
fear itself,
For panic is but a feeling based on
emotion without fact.
If I try to control it through willpower
and force it to stop,
I find it grows stronger and feeds on
my efforts to control.
If I accept it and understand in time
it will pass,
It becomes weaker as I let go of my
worry thoughts.
It would be nice to never experience
panic again,
But I take comfort in knowing that it is
simply a bag of wind.

1. Have you experienced panic attacks, or do you know someone near to your heart who does?

2. Have you learned that taking slow, deep breaths for several moments helps calm one's physiology?

3. What are common worry thoughts that tend to fuel panic attacks?

4. What steps might one take to reduce their chances of experiencing panic attacks?

5. What message is the author trying to convey by referring to panic attacks as a bag of wind?

REFLECTIONS OF THE AUTHOR

Panic attacks affect many people, and they can lead some to fear leaving their home or carrying on normal activities of daily living. Although a person understands their fear is unreasonable, it feels as real as if the person's life was being threatened. It is important for the struggling person to understand that panic attacks are uncomfortable, but not dangerous.

In writing this poem, I want to validate how frightening and difficult panic attacks are. Common beliefs that intensify panic attacks include:

- ☐ I'm having a heart attack. I'm dying.
- ☐ I can't breathe.
- ☐ I'm losing my mind.
- ☐ I'm making a fool of myself.

It helps a person to recognize they are simply having a panic attack, and that in time it will pass. Taking slow and deep breaths frequently triggers the relaxation response and helps them to pass more quickly. Talking with a supportive friend or family member often is beneficial to the person experiencing one.

I hope this poem will give you some insight into what persons often go through when they have panic attacks. If you have them, consider seeing a therapist to learn effective coping skills. If you know someone who experiences panic attacks, be supportive and encourage them to seek help.

1. Write about a time in your life when you were frightened.

_____

_____

_____

_____

2. What are steps you take to calm down when you feel overly anxious or panic?

_____

_____

_____

_____

3. Write about what you might do to support someone who struggles with excessive anxiety.

_____

_____

_____

_____

§

~ *Taming Emotions* ~

It makes no sense to think you should
not feel how you feel.
Emotions are simply a physical response to
what you sense and think.

There are healthy ways to tame the intensity
of your feelings,
But be aware that numbing and stuffing may
make things worse.

Way too often persons judge themselves
for having feelings,
And their judgments trigger a chain
of undesired events.

Understanding that all of your emotions
serve a purpose,
And that anger is neither good or bad
is helpful knowledge.

Accepting that emotions are an important
part of life,
And thoughts intensify or decrease them
gives us control.

Assuming the worst often leads to
fear and anger,
While assuming the best can bring
some peace of mind.

There are times to take deep breaths and
times to go for walks,
And we must tend to the body in order to
quiet the mind.

Let go of perfection, judgments and the
need to be right,
And you will begin to experience success
in taming your emotions.

QUESTIONS TO PONDER

1. What are some body sensations you have when you feel a particular way? Do your fists clinch when you're angry, or do you experience lightness in your chest when you're happy?

2. What do you do that intensifies unwanted emotions?

3. What do you do at times that helps you to savor desired emotions?

4. How can changing your thoughts help you control your feelings?

5. Do you believe letting go of perfectionism, judgments, and the need to be right could help tame your emotions?

REFLECTIONS OF THE AUTHOR

"Name it to tame it" is a saying often used in helping persons better manage their emotions. Pausing for a second to identify what emotion you are experiencing, can be an important first step in better controlling your emotions.

In writing the poem, "Taming Emotions", I wanted to convey that it is not wrong or bad to experience feelings. It often creates more problems when a person thinks, "It is wrong of me to feel that way, I should feel differently." Don't blame yourself for feeling angry but be careful to not fuel your anger by making a multitude of irrational assumptions and negative judgments.

You can learn to better manage your feelings by taking steps to make physiological changes in your body. When anxious, taking slow and deep breaths can help you to quiet your body and mind. When sad, being more active and spending time with supportive people can improve your mood.

I hope that this poem will help you to understand that you often have more control over your feelings than you think.

1. What emotion tends to cause you the most problems?

_____

_____

_____

2. Write about what steps you might take to better manage that feeling.

_____

_____

_____

3. Journal briefly about how letting go of perfectionism, judgments, and the need to be right could help you to better manage your emotions.

_____

_____

_____

_____

§

~ *Letting Go of Guilt and Shame* ~

For countless years I believed I was to blame
for making others angry and hurt,
But now I realize I'm not the cause for how
others feel or what they do.
I allowed them to convince me that my actions could
stress another enough to die,
Until I began to see how their judgments and
blame created their own stress.
I believed I should always give in to any
demands placed on me,
And failure to please others led me
to feel overwhelming guilt.
It is clear that I was simply being manipulated
by countless guilt trips,
And now I'm free to not take on their demands
or to feel unjustified guilt.
Persons create their own stress by thoughts
and ways they live,
So I choose to stop allowing others to control
me through blame.
I alone am responsible for my thoughts,
feelings, and actions,
And to the extent I believe this, I will be able
to find happiness and peace.

1. Have you struggled with feelings of guilt and/or shame?
2. Has anyone in your life used guilt trips over and over to manipulate you?
3. Do you find yourself at times using guilt to try to get your way?
4. What have you done to free yourself from the manipulation of others?
5. Do you frequently feel victimized, or have you discovered that taking responsibility for your thoughts and feelings has freed you?

REFLECTIONS OF THE AUTHOR

Guilt and shame are powerful emotions. Some guilt serves the purpose of being a deterrent to hurting others. Excessive feelings of guilt and shame tend to be self-limiting and cause a person to become depressed and stuck in a pattern of self-defeating behavior.

I believe that guilt and shame are frequently learned and have been used by persons in authority to control others. Parents, teachers and others have throughout time shamed persons to make them feel bad, so they won't continue to repeat an undesired behavior. Unfortunately, some individuals become hyper-sensitive to shame, and over time view themselves as being bad and unworthy.

This poem was written for persons who tend to feel guilty or shameful when it is not warranted. It encourages such persons to become aware of guilt trips and to stop buying into them. It conveys that we cannot control the feelings of others, and that often when persons blame us for their feelings, they are failing to accept responsibility for their own thoughts and actions.

I hope this poem proves helpful to you if you are prone to feel guilt or shame easily. It may be helpful for you to talk with others who also struggle with feelings of excessive guilt.

1. Write about a time when you have felt unjustified shame or guilt.

_____

_____

_____

2. Briefly write about someone who uses guilt trips to try to control others.

_____

_____

_____

_____

3. What steps could you take to be less influenced by others who tend to trigger you to feel bad?

_____

_____

_____

_____

§

Notes

_____

_____

_____

_____

_____

_____

_____

_____

_____

_____

_____

_____

RECOVERING FROM PAINFUL EXPERIENCES

Poems in this section relate to recovering from painful experiences and choosing life over suicide. The five poems teach ideas for going on after trauma, the power that comes from letting go, the importance of not giving into self-harm, the value of accepting that change is a part of life, and the struggle of accepting death of a loved one.

In life there are times when we feel that there will be
no end to the pain we endure.
After suffering emotional hurt and fear for so long,
it is easy to despair.
Yet many find it most difficult to face life after the
crisis has passed.
It may be because our trust in God, in others or
in ourselves has been broken.
To resolve this issue of trust we must be willing to
look at what role we played.
So often we have allowed things to happen that
we needed to stop.
By seeing the part we played in the problem,
we can feel less a victim.
It is helpful to see that at any time we can choose
to act in a loving way.
This does not mean that we allow another to act
in an abusive manner.
We cannot change anyone, but we can choose to
act assertively and wisely.
Anxiety can rob us of any happiness we find today
by living in fear of the future.
Worry never helps us to change the future —
it only destroys our peace of mind.
Thoughtful planning may help avert future problems,
but worry just keeps us spinning our wheels.
At other times we obsess about past hurtful
events we cannot change.
We can learn from the past and accept the fact
we can never change it.

Acceptance is the key for discovering peace of mind
and changing how we live.
Acceptance is realizing we cannot control the future
or change a single thing that is past.
With acceptance we understand we can handle
any crisis with dignity.
Acceptance, trust, and hope are the virtues that
allow us to go on after the trauma.

1. Have you experienced a time in your life where you were overwhelmed by a difficult situation?

2. Why is it at times difficult to move forward after surviving a crisis?

3. Have you been so hurt that it has made it difficult to trust anyone?

4. Do you worry too much and allow the fear of the future to rob you of peace of mind in the present?

5. How does the acceptance of "what is" help you to better handle life?

REFLECTIONS OF THE AUTHOR

Emotional trauma can have a profound impact on a person's life. Persons suffering from traumatic experiences are often overwhelmed by intense anxiety and even panic. They may be in the fight-flight response much of the time.

It is difficult for most people who have not lived through intensely painful experiences to understand how life can remain difficult far after the crisis has passed. "Going on After Trauma" is a poem that explores some of the reasons why life may continue to be difficult after the painful event is over.

This poem also points to the importance of acceptance, trust, and hope in rebounding from a traumatic event. It warns about the futility of getting caught up in our worry thoughts. It explains how acceptance is the key to finding peace of mind. If you have been through emotionally traumatic times, I hope this poem can provide some peace of mind and hope to you.

1. Write about how some trauma or painful experience has had a
    negative impact on your life.

_____

_____

_____

2. How have you been affected by the experience long after it was
    over?

_____

_____

_____

3. Write about steps you feel you might take to help you heal from
    or overcome a past painful event.

_____

_____

_____

§

~ Letting Go ~

One of the most difficult tasks in life
is letting go.
As long as we're tied to the dock
we cannot sail.
It is sad to see persons so tied
to the past,
They are unable to enjoy the present
or relish tomorrow.
Certainly life offers us many opportunities
for letting go.
To take our first step we must
courageously let go.
We cannot enter kindergarten without
leaving home.
To become more independent we must
venture from our family.
Letting go of one we love is a most
difficult challenge.
Sometimes death takes away one
we dearly love.
Loss may also come from relocation,
separation and divorce.
Letting go requires time and work
to heal our hurt,
But refusing to let go is unwise and
approaches insanity.
We need to accept letting go is a difficult,
but a most necessary step.

QUESTIONS TO PONDER

1. What is meant by the following phrase?
   "As long as we are tied to the dock we cannot sail."

2. How much of your time is spent brooding about the past or worrying about the future?

3. Have you had to struggle with the loss of a loved one?

4. Do you approach letting go with courage, or do you approach it screaming and kicking?

5. What is meant by the concluding line of this poem?
   "We need to accept letting go is a difficult, but a most necessary step."

REFLECTIONS OF THE AUTHOR

I believe there is healing power in letting go. I have witnessed much relief and comfort in clients who have been able to forgive others for hurtful things they have done. Forgiveness does not mean that abusive actions were okay or deserved, but it does mean that a person does not have to continue replaying those hurtful events in their mind, perpetuating the pain.

Some become overly attached to possessions and letting go of that attachment allows them to begin to love others more and things less. Many suffer from their attachment to unhealthy beliefs and judgments. All-or-nothing thinking can create a lot of stress and anger when others do not think or act the way we think they should. Again, letting go can be emotionally freeing and often improves our relationships with others.

It is my hope that reading the "Letting Go" poem will encourage you to release whatever keeps you locked into self-defeating patterns of behavior. Throughout life there are countless things that we need to let go to grow, and at the same time there are other ways that we need to remain steady and consistent. Take a moment to think about something you need to let go of that would be beneficial to your growth and happiness.

1. Write about worries or painful memories that you need to let go of to be happier and at peace.

_____

_____

_____

2. Write about something that you let go of that made you feel better.

_____

_____

_____

3. Write about someone you know who experiences suffering because they refuse to let go.

_____

_____

_____

§

~ *Choose Life* ~

My dear friend, I know you hear
death calling —
Telling you that it is no longer
worth going on.
It lies to you and whispers that
you're worthless —
And have nothing of value to
give this world.

You have shared your heart and
pain with me,
And I understand how deeply
hurt you are.
If it were not for your big heart and
exceeding sensitivity,
Death would not so easily deceive
and snare you.

Again and again death tells you
vicious lies like —
No one cares or would be heartbroken
if you were to die.
I fear in your despair and confusion
you may believe
This sad delusion that deeply hurts
and is so untrue.

In the darkness of your crippling
depression,
It is quite hard for you to
clearly see.
I ask for my sake that you
please wait
For dawn's light to show
a better way.

Although you believe your heart to be
broken beyond repair,
I can see it has just been stretched
to make room for healing.
At the light of day you may see
things differently,
And realize you have more to learn
and more to give.

Trust me to help you through
the night.
Hold my hand and together
we will cry.
Death does not wish you to
discover
How precious you truly are
to others.

Choose life and bravely confront
death's lies,
And in so doing you will find hope
to help you go on.
Believe in the healing power
of love,
And then you will embrace the
strength you need.

You alone have a special
gift to share.
Imagine in your mind your
own unique purpose.
Open your stretched heart to love's
healing power,
And lean on me, my friend, for as
long as you need.

1. Some say suicide is a permanent solution to a temporary problem. Do you agree or disagree?

2. Do you think that most people who commit suicide are confused and fail to see that they have much to give?

3. Why is it so hard to realize that things will get better when a person is deeply depressed and suicidal?

4. How does suicide affect family members and friends of the one who took their life?

5. What do you think a person who feels suicidal needs in order to choose life?

REFLECTIONS OF THE AUTHOR

I wrote "Choose Life" on the morning of the funeral of my sixteen-year-old great niece who took her life. I want to help persons find the courage to choose life over suicide when they feel hopeless and are in deep despair. I believe many are not able to clearly think nor see that the severe pain of depression will not always be there.

As a therapist, I believe more can be done to help persons who are suicidal. In some respects, depression is a thought disorder. Almost all of the suicidal clients I have worked with have a distorted self-image. When feeling suicidal, they have been overly self-critical and magnify their faults, and at the same time tend to be totally blind to their compassionate heart and many strengths.

I hope that much more will be done to provide help for persons who struggle with depression and feelings of worthlessness. We need to find a way to empower people to confront the lies they believe in their minds, and to free them to become the valued persons they are intended to be.

1. Write briefly about one of the darkest hours you have
    experienced in your life.

    _____

    _____

    _____

    _____

2. Did the thought of suicide raise its ugly head? What helped you
    work through this difficult time?

    _____

    _____

    _____

    _____

    _____

3. Write about something you feel could be done to help a person
    when they feel suicidal.

    _____

    _____

    _____

    _____

§

~ Change is a Part of Life ~

All too often it is tempting to crawl into a hole
and refuse to change,
But we do not have the choice to change whether
we like it or not.
Change is as much a part of our existence as
is breathing air.
The tide comes and goes and the earth spins
on its axis
Bringing both the light of day and the
darkness of night.
We can only choose how we are to meet
change when it comes.
We can bury our head in the sand or complain
about things not being the same.
I believe it is wise to meet change with an
open mind and caution.
It is often helpful to see the true intentions
underlying the change
Before one jumps quickly to one side of
the fence or the other.
We cannot stop change or control others,
but we can respond wisely.
I hope that in looking back when my life
nears completion,
I see for the most part I faced change with
courage and dignity.

1. Do you tend to dread or welcome change?

2. What are some anticipated changes that you are currently looking forward to?

3. Why is it important to accept that change is a part of life?

4. Do you find yourself fighting change and wishing things were the way they used to be?

5. What can you do to deal with change in a more positive way?

REFLECTIONS OF THE AUTHOR

Change is very much a part of all of our lives. If we fear change, we can spend much of our time caught up in worry and feelings of anxiety. If we welcome change, we will be free to experience hope and pleasant anticipation. Our outlook truly has more to do with our attitude and faith than it does with the external events that occur in our life.

I hope my poem will help you to accept that change is inevitable and encourage you to embrace it as an important part of life. As a therapist I teach my clients that therapy revolves around two principles of change. We can change how we think and in time, changes in thought will lead to changes in our feelings and what we do. The second thing we can do is to change our actions, and this in time will lead to changes in both our beliefs and feelings.

Decide today that change cannot be stopped or avoided for long. Make the choice to welcome it into your life, and approach it with both an open mind and some caution. Focus on facing change with courage and dignity. If you do this, you will experience more happiness and peace of mind.

1. Write briefly about your typical response to change.

_____

_____

_____

_____

2. How would you like to respond to change differently?

_____

_____

_____

3. Write down some simple things you can do to respond to change
    in a positive way.

_____

_____

_____

_____

§

~ *On Angel's Wings* ~

If I could send a letter on angel's wings
To heaven above where angels sing,
I would tell you how much you're missed,
And I would send my love with a kiss.

Let me tell you from the depth of my heart
How sad and hurt I felt when you did part.
At first I believed I would never again smile,
For without you nothing seemed worthwhile.

At times tears filled my weeping eyes,
As I struggled to tell reality from lies.
Ever so slowly the time did pass
And one day I did again smile at last.

Initially I felt so guilty for just having fun,
For simply enjoying the warmth of the sun.
But the darkness of night gives way to dawn,
And I know deep down you want me to go on.

Gradually with the passing of time I find
The will to live and peace of mind.
Sweet memories of loving times shared
Would my letter sent on angel's wings bear.

Letting you know I must and I will go on
Even though a precious part of my life is gone.
Comfort I find knowing you'll always be a part
Of my life for your love lives on in my heart.

1. Have you lost someone you deeply loved?

2. While grieving, have you felt like you would never feel happy again?

3. Have there been times when you felt guilty because you were having a good time?

4. What has helped you to heal from grief?

5. Does someone you loved and lost live on in in your heart?

REFLECTIONS OF THE AUTHOR

I wrote "On Angel's Wings" to help clients understand that most persons are really thrown when they lose someone they deeply love, especially if the person died unexpectedly. I tried to capture some of the feelings I read about from reading I had done pertaining to grief.

Death is a part of life, and if we live long enough, we will surely lose family and friends who have been dear to us. I hope you will feel free to share this with others who are grieving, if you believe it can bring some comfort to that person.

I have found that it helps me to focus more on positive times I've shared with someone I love when they die, instead of ruminating about their final days when they were possibly quite ill and in pain. Don't try to block out the painful memories, but simply accept what has been and be grateful for the happy memories you have. Find comfort in knowing that person will live on in your heart.

1. Write about how you experienced grief when someone you
   loved died.

   _____

   _____

   _____

   _____

2. What emotions did you feel? Were you angry, sad, devastated,
   accepting, fearful, or guilty?

   _____

   _____

   _____

3. Write about what helped you to gradually heal and find the
   strength to continue on with your life.

   _____

   _____

   _____

   _____

§

_____

_____

_____

_____

_____

_____

_____

_____

_____

_____

_____

_____

_____

INTERPERSONAL HEALTH

Poetry from this section of the workbook relates to universal truths you need to understand to have better relationships and to not be manipulated by others. The first poem in this section points out the benefit of spending time with persons who are positive and validating. Other poems explain the value of being a good listener, the importance of encouragement, the benefit of humor, and the need to avoid trying to please everyone all of the time.

~ Bobbers and Sinkers ~

In life there are two types of people —
bobbers and sinkers.
Bobbers are persons who listen and encourage
while sinkers are just stinkers.
Sinkers always look for the worst in others
and skillfully bring it out.
They judge, blame, manipulate with guilt,
and scream and shout.
Sinkers themselves feel so low they never wish
to see another rise,
So their negative outlook and harsh criticism
are of little surprise.
Bobbers are the people I truly want to
hang around,
Because acceptance and good humor
in them abound.
No matter how discouraged and frustrated
you may feel,
Bobbers lift you up with encouragement
that is genuine and real.
Unless you want to sink to the bottom and
settle into mire,
I suggest you seek out bobbers —
affirming persons you admire.

QUESTIONS TO PONDER

1. Who do you hang out with that lifts your spirits and encourages you?

2. Who are you around that typically takes the wind out of your sails?

3. What can you do to limit the negative effect that some people have on you?

4. Who do you need to spend less time with?

5. What steps might you take to be around positive people more often?

REFLECTIONS OF THE AUTHOR

I often use the "Bobbers and Sinkers" poem with clients who are struggling with persons who are overly critical and negative. After they read it, they often become aware of how they are allowing others to affect them in an unhealthy way. When they mention being hurt by another, I ask them if the person is a sinker. I will comment on positive persons they mention as being bobbers.

I try to help clients understand that others cannot hurt them by critical words and guilt trips, if they don't buy into others' negativity. It is not what others say, but rather what one believes that causes him or her emotional pain.

I love to fish, so I am quite familiar with bobbers, sinkers and other tackle. I hope reading this poem encourages you to search out more bobbers and to distance yourself from sinkers.

1. Write about someone who is or has been a bobber in your life. How has this person lifted your spirits?

_____

_____

_____

2. Write about why you think a particular sinker in your life is the way he or she is.

_____

_____

_____

3. Write about how you would like to handle the critical words of others in the future.

_____

_____

_____

§

~ *Listening is a Gift of Love* ~

When I feel depressed and quite lonely,
all I really need is for someone to listen.
True listening is putting all else aside
to completely be there with the other person.
You cannot deeply listen if you're watching TV
or looking up occasionally from a novel.
Genuine listening demands your full attention
and a willingness to feel what I feel.
You may hold my hand when you listen,
but I actually need you to hold my heart.
My heart will be comforted by your understanding,
and it may be further broken by rejection.
I must be careful in whom I choose to hold
my heart and listen to my dreams.
It would be foolish to open up to someone who
has little interest and doesn't care.
If you want to be close to me and my heart,
you will need to show genuine caring.
When listening, put me first in your thoughts,
and do your best to not be defensive.
Unless you are willing to try to understand me,
I will be unable to find courage to be honest.
Realize that just as listening is a gift of love,
so too is sharing one's true feelings.

QUESTIONS TO PONDER

1. When you feel sad and lonely, what do you want from a friend or loved one?

2. What is involved in giving someone your undivided attention?

3. Are there times when it would be nice for someone to listen and hold your heart?

4. Have you shared something with someone and later felt foolish for trusting that person?

5. Do you believe that deep listening is a gift of love?

REFLECTIONS OF THE AUTHOR

Listening is an essential part of therapy and of healthy relationships. It is truly a gift of love. Unfortunately, there are many obstacles that hinder deep listening, and we need to be aware and take steps to overcome them.

Failure to see things from anyone's perspective other than our own is a common roadblock to listening. "Should thinking" is another hindrance. Distractions are so prevalent in our busy lives and they frequently interfere with genuine listening.

I hope that my poem, "Listening is a Gift of Love", will provide you with a better understanding of the importance of deep listening and what it entails. During this week make a concerted effort to listen deeply to others. Observe what happens when you become fully involved in listening. Listen as if you are actually holding the emotional heart of the one you are trying your best to understand and validate.

1. Write about ways in which you are a good listener.

_____

_____

_____

2. Write about a time when you did a poor job of listening. What got in your way?

_____

_____

_____

3. Journal about what you feel you need to do to be a better listener.

_____

_____

_____

§

~ *Encourage Me* ~

Of all the gifts you've given me, I value most
your encouragement.
We each like to be encouraged by those
who really care.
It is much easier to face life's difficulties when
others believe in us.
It is as though your positive expectations
bring out my best.
Thank you for those times you have spoken
of my strengths.
Thank you for believing in me when I could not
believe in myself.
Thank you for simply being there when
no one else was.
Thank you for seeing beyond my weaknesses
into my loving heart.
Thank you for telling me life is hard and
I would make it through.
Thank you for the nod that said I could go on
when I wanted to turn back.
Thank you for the warm hug to congratulate me
on a job well done.
You have made my life so much better by
simply believing in me.
I welcome your continued support and will
always be grateful to you.

QUESTIONS TO PONDER

1. How do you feel when someone genuinely encourages you?

2. How do you like to be encouraged?

3. Who is someone who has been a positive person in your life and believes in you?

4. How do you show encouragement to others?

5. What steps could you take to improve giving encouragement to others?

REFLECTIONS OF THE AUTHOR

I believe strongly in the power of positive expectations and encouragement. The "Encourage Me" poem is written to convey to my clients and readers that we all need encouragement, and we connect with others when we bless them with words of kindness and validation. The essence of encouragement is the ability to see and recognize the good in other people.

The poem identifies many aspects of encouragement. Showing belief in others, conveying positive expectations, recognizing strengths, being there when needed, being supportive, and validating a job well done are all ways in which we can show encouragement. Encouragement is to a person what sunshine is to a plant — it promotes growth.

If you love someone, show him or her encouragement. If you want a person to grow in confidence, show him or her encouragement. If you want to build friendships, then show others encouragement. If others give you encouragement, do not discount their praise. Accept it and say thank you.

1. Write about someone in your life who has believed in you and shown you encouragement.

_____

_____

_____

_____

2. Write about the ways you encourage others, and how you feel after speaking words of validation.

_____

_____

_____

_____

3. Write about someone who needs your encouragement. How could you show it?

_____

_____

_____

_____

_____

§

~ *Humor is Good Medicine* ~

Of all the gifts God has blessed me with,
my sense of humor is most precious.
There are few problems encountered in life
that cannot be lessened with humor.
Laughter at times ends the deafening silence
and helps to dry away our tears.
In therapy the greatest healing force is
the ability to laugh at oneself.
Defensiveness between two angry persons
can quickly end with good humor.
Is there a better remedy for boredom
than doing something funny?
Humor opens our eyes to clearly see
our problems can't be that big.
Even when one must ultimately face death,
humor can make it less terrifying.
Humor is to life what lubricant is to a
new car or old truck.
It reduces the friction of stress and hurt
allowing us to travel farther.
Let me lose almost any other gift,
before I lose my sense of humor.

1. What are things that make you laugh?

2. Who do you know that uses humor to better cope with difficulties of life?

3. How do you use humor to ease tensions?

4. Do you use humor defensively to avoid talking about serious issues?

5. What might you do to use humor more often to bring a smile to others?

REFLECTIONS OF THE AUTHOR

I am frequently amazed by my clients who struggle with horrific events and plod through them with humor and a sense of hope. I don't know where they muster the courage to fight on bravely in spite of being overwhelmed by the traumas and tragedies. It seems that humor is their shield that prevents the arrows of life from rupturing their heart.

As a young psychologist, I purchased a book written on how to use humor in therapy. It did not make me laugh, and after reading less than a quarter of the book, I gave up on it. I would find it difficult to put into words how I use humor with clients. It is something that spontaneously happens when I am mindfully listening to a person talk about their pain. I don't think it can be strategically planned and executed.

I hope you enjoy reading "Humor is Good Medicine". I am more likely to share it with a client who has a healthy sense of humor to validate them, than I am with a client that shows little or no humor. If you have a good sense of humor, be grateful for it. If you lack humor, loosen up a little and make more time to have fun.

1. Write about how humor has helped you through a tough time.

_____

_____

_____

_____

2. What are things you do that commonly bring happiness and
   laughter to you?

_____

_____

_____

3. How do you at times use humor to be supportive of others you
   love?

_____

_____

_____

§

~ *Pleasing can be Costly* ~

Many go through life with the mistaken belief that
they must make everyone happy,
And for their efforts they are rewarded with ulcers
and disrespect of most everyone.
Persons who try too hard miserably fail to make
anyone happy including oneself,
And as their resentment grows they often inflict
feelings of guilt on those near.
How can one make others happy if one has not
discovered happiness himself?
Painfully the answer is that one cannot find
happiness in denying oneself,
And there can be little lasting happiness without
peace of mind.
Persons seldom respect anyone who simply says
what others want to hear,
For respect is built on honesty and on the courage
to act in a way that is true.
Leave pleasing to the politicians and seek to be
a real person,
Who takes responsibility for how you choose to
think, feel and act.
This way you will become less attractive to those
who like to manipulate,
And more appealing to others who too are seeking
to be honest and real.

79

QUESTIONS TO PONDER

1. Do you try too hard to make others happy?

2. Do you try to avoid conflict and in doing so fail to stand up for what you believe is right?

3. Have you noticed that people who sacrifice often tend to feel resentment?

4. Do you agree with the statement that persons seldom respect anyone who simply says what others want to hear?

5. What is meant by the statement?
   "Leave pleasing to the politicians and seek to be a real person."

REFLECTIONS OF THE AUTHOR

As a therapist, I have observed that perfectionism and pleasing are two irrational beliefs that create much distress in the lives of many. Certainly, there is a positive side to pleasing, but trying too hard to please others creates a lot of anxiety and may create interpersonal problems.

I often share this poem with clients that struggle with trying to please everyone. In the poem I point out that pleasers are often rewarded with ulcers and disrespect. Readers are encouraged to be true to themselves and to make time to find happiness by caring for oneself.

All too often persons who play the martyr role express anger toward those they have intended to help. It is far better to show faith in others and convey positive expectations than to do things for others that they are quite capable of doing themselves. I hope reading "Pleasing can be Costly" will cause you to pause and think twice before you try too hard to please others.

1. Write about a time when you tried too hard to please others and you ended up regretting it.

_____

_____

_____

_____

2. Write about when pleasing is a good thing for both others and you.

_____

_____

_____

_____

3. Write about what you need to do to avoid trying too hard to please others.

_____

_____

_____

_____

§

_____

_____

_____

_____

_____

_____

_____

_____

_____

_____

_____

_____

_____

_____

_____

_____

_____

_____

_____

FINDING HAPPINESS

This part of the poetry workbook shows ways to find more happiness in life. The first poem in this section suggests simple ways to discover more joy and happiness. Others discuss the wonder of being a parent, the value of smiling, the power of our thoughts in experiencing happiness and peace of mind, and how gratitude contributes to a more joyful life.

~ *Happiness* ~

If I tried to define happiness, I'm sure
I would lose some of it.
It cannot be caught and held captive in a jar,
like a firefly brightly lit.

Happiness is always a welcome friend that
makes life brighter,
And it seems to come when I'm less serious –
when things are seen lighter.

I cannot wait on the couch and just hope
it will magically appear,
For it's not something I'm simply entitled to
and this is clear.

I cannot win it in a lottery or buy it
with a lot of money,
And I'm more likely to find it by doing
something funny.

Sometimes it comes to me when I've
completed work,
And at other times it may visit me when I
meet a friendly clerk.

If in my selfishness I try to hide it away
and keep it all to myself,
It quickly disappears as does a leprechaun
or frightened little elf.

When I share it with family and friends
and freely give it away,
Happiness grows stronger and I find
more time for play.

I have learned to appreciate happiness
for what it is.
Like Alka-Seltzer in a glass of water —
it gives life its fizz.

1. Is happiness something that is easy to find or to develop?

2. What have you done in the past that has helped you to experience happiness?

3. Do you believe happiness automatically comes with having lots of money?

4. When you try to keep happiness to yourself, does it grow or soon disappear?

5. How does an attitude of gratitude affect your happiness?

REFLECTIONS OF THE AUTHOR

I share this poem with clients when I want them to smile or when I am teaching them about ways to experience more happiness. The school of positive psychology has much to offer regarding the study of happiness. For instance, the daily exercise of writing down three new things each day that one is grateful for increases happiness by focusing more on the positive.

The following are just a few things an individual can do to cultivate happiness:

☐ Do an act of kindness
☐ Engage in exercise
☐ Plan something fun to do
☐ Send someone a gratitude letter
☐ Speak words of encouragement
☐ Go for a nature walk on a nice day
☐ Play with or hold your pet
☐ Look at pictures of loved ones

I hope my poem on happiness made you smile or chuckle. Remember that happiness grows when we give it away. It also tends to appear when we are playful.

1. Write about a really happy time in your life.

_____

_____

_____

_____

2. Have you experienced times when you felt you would never be happy again? What happened?

_____

_____

_____

_____

3. Write about things you do that frequently help you feel happier.

_____

_____

_____

_____

§

~ *Children are Precious Gifts* ~

Children are precious gifts from above,
With whom we are blessed to enjoy and love.
They warm our hearts with hugs and smiles,
Even though they present us with many trials.

If we make time for them to spend in play,
They will make time for us some future day.
If we listen to how they think and feel,
They will open up to us and be real.

In discipline we must follow through,
So they can count on what we will do.
Through consistency is built faith and trust,
And keeping promises to a child is a must.

Nagging and threatening does no good,
And leads to frustration in parenthood.
By conveying faith in who they are,
We will give them courage to go far.

By giving them our undivided time,
We will see their self-esteem climb.
Most important of all in what we do,
Is to convey our love and be true.

1. Do you enjoy being around children? Why?

2. What can parents do to make it more likely their children will be close to them?

3. Why is it important for parents to follow through with what they say they will do?

4. Why is threatening and nagging at kids ineffective?

5. Do you believe it is vital for parents to show love to their children?

REFLECTIONS OF THE AUTHOR

Children who are seen by their parents as being gifts from above are fortunate. As a therapist, I have worked with many persons who were not shown love and support by their parents. Those who have grown up with significant childhood neglect and abuse start life with a major disadvantage.

"Children are Precious Gifts" was written to recognize the importance of unconditional love in parenting. Healthy parents are able to show both love and discipline, and both are essential for positive child development. Love helps children to trust and to develop the courage to take positive risks. Discipline helps children to respect others and to get along in society.

If parents want to have a good relationship with their children, they will need to devote time to them. Parents will feel less resentment if they make time to play with their kids and enjoy them. I hope my poem will help you to value the beauty and wonder of children and the importance of being a loving and strong parent.

1. In what ways were you shown love and caring by your parents?

_____

_____

_____

_____

2. If you are a parent, what are some of your favorite things you like to do with your child or children?

_____

_____

_____

_____

3. Write about what you believe are the most important qualities of a good parent.

_____

_____

_____

_____

§

~ *Smiles have Healing Power* ~

As you share your painful story,
tears gently flow from your eyes.
Yet a smile curves your lips,
and I realize it's not a disguise.

You have experienced trauma,
and a life time of abuse.
But there is strength within you,
and victimhood you refuse.

Armed with gratitude and humor,
a wonderful smile lights your face.
You have learned that pain
need not keep you from grace.

Although you've been deeply wronged,
you do not hold a grudge.
You have found the power to forgive,
and you no longer judge.

As you've learned to accept reality,
your sense of humor has grown.
All human souls are at times afraid
and broken — this is known.

You have discovered that humor
has much healing power.
And your beautiful smile is testimony
that you are truly empowered.

1. What struggles have you overcome in your life?
2. Have you been mentally, physically or sexually abused?
3. What traumas or painful experiences have you had to face?
4. Are you free to genuinely smile and confide in trusted others?
5. Have you developed a sense of humor and the capacity to laugh at yourself?

REFLECTIONS OF THE AUTHOR

In all honesty, I have not shared this poem with many clients. It is one of many that was written and forgotten. I believe it would be quite appropriate to share with any client who has struggled and learned the power of humor and gratitude. I have had several PTSD clients that may have benefited from reading it.

Have you ever noticed how a genuine smile eases tension and almost immediately lifts one's spirit? We want to be around persons who smile because they bring energy into a room.

Genuine smiles and humor are often missing when a person is stuck in a cycle of negativity and victimhood. Most therapists would agree that it is easier to work with clients who are able to laugh at themselves and the ridiculous events that take place in life. Possibly compassion, honesty, and a helping relationship can over time empower persons who have not yet learned the beauty of a simple smile.

1. Write about someone who has struggled and yet has a wonderful smile.

_____

_____

_____

_____

2. What have others told you about your smile and your sense of humor?

_____

_____

_____

_____

3. Write about how the power to forgive or learning to be less judgmental helps one to smile.

_____

_____

_____

_____

§

~ *Master of My Mind* ~

Oh what great power I do hold
in my very own mind.
I alone am master of my thoughts
and keeper of my heart.

I once was a leaf blowing in the wind
before opening my eyes.
In morning light I could clearly see
I control my every thought.

With open hands and a gentle smile
I let go of fear.
My anxious foe was only an illusion
made of worry thoughts.

Anger has little place in my life for
I no longer judge.
Instead I hold compassion in my heart
and anger disappears.

For years I was bound to shame,
but now I'm set free.
I no longer believe the blaming words
I once embraced.

Now I am quick to feel happiness —
often I feel at peace.
I am the master of my mind and
I'm most grateful.

1. How well do you control your thoughts?

2. What is the relationship between your worry thoughts and fear?

3. Have you learned to not hold on to anger?

4. Do you frequently experience feelings of shame, or have you learned to let go of self-blame?

5. What steps might you take to do a better job of being master of your mind?

REFLECTIONS OF THE AUTHOR

My favorite quote is actually from Henry Ford. It is: "Think you can — think you can't — either way you're right." I believe that our thoughts are powerful, and that what we believe largely determines how we feel and what we do.

Many of the women and men I see in therapy suffer emotional pain more from how they think than what has actually happened to them. Some have had horrific experiences, but it is the holding onto negative interpretations of those events that cause most of their pain. So often they have come to believe they are "damaged goods," they are "bad," or they are "worthless and incapable."

I believe being in a caring relationship makes it possible to see oneself in a new light, and to gradually replace the highly critical self-image with a compassionate and positive one. This poem can be used to suggest that we are capable of changing who we are by first seeing oneself as he or she wants to be.

1. Write how your negative thoughts prevent you from being the person you want to be.

_____

_____

_____

2. What are the most important negative beliefs you need to work on changing?

_____

_____

_____

3. In the few lines below, write about the person you want to be. Start each sentence with: "I am...."

_____

_____

_____

_____

§

~ *Gratitude is a Precious Gift* ~

Gratitude is a most precious gift
so easily given,
And is powerful in lifting the spirits
of another.
To smile and express appreciation
takes so little time,
And yet it is long remembered by
the receiving party.
When you have given a gift,
a gracious acknowledgement
Is welcomed and assures your
giving was worthwhile.
Recognizing a caring act shown
by a friend
Can do much to strengthen a
valued friendship.
Reach out and express gratitude at
any opportunity,
And you will find your life richer
for doing so.

1. Do you see a relationship between being grateful and feeling happy?

2. How do you feel when you do something nice for another person?

3. How do you respond when someone does something nice for you?

4. Do you believe that the expression of gratitude strengthens relationships?

5. Who do you know that often expresses gratitude? Is that person liked by others?

REFLECTIONS OF THE AUTHOR

Gratitude is something that everyone needs to practice on a daily basis. It is my belief that gratitude is a good antidote for both depression and anxiety. We worry less when we are grateful for our blessings, and we are happier.

"Gratitude is a Precious Gift" conveys many simple truths about gratitude. It is easily given. It takes so little time to smile and say thank you. Acts of showing appreciation are often remembered for some time. Being thankful does strengthen friendships and family relationships. Persons expressing gratitude do tend to enjoy a richer emotional life.

As a therapist, I often encourage my clients to practice gratitude. I sometimes assign clients to complete a "Silver Lining Worksheet." In doing so they write one sentence expressing how they feel about a recent difficult event, and then they write a sentence identifying something they are grateful for that has come from that event. Learning to look for something positive that comes out of a painful experience helps us to develop resilience.

1. Write about several things you are grateful to experience.

_____

_____

_____

_____

2. Write about ways you express appreciation to others. How do you feel when you show gratitude?

_____

_____

_____

_____

3. Write about one thing you could do to express or experience more gratitude.

_____

_____

_____

§

Notes

DIALECTICAL BEHAVIOR THERAPY

Dialectical Behavior Therapy (DBT) is a treatment found to be quite helpful for persons who tend to be over-reactive and lose control of their emotions and actions when triggered. Many persons who need this treatment often feel life isn't worth living. DBT was developed by Marsha Linehan, Ph.D., psychologist, researcher and therapist.

The poems in this section focus on five important skills that are relevant to anyone who wants to improve his or her life. The poems relate to core areas of teaching in DBT. The areas are:

Mindfulness
Interpersonal Effectiveness
Emotional Regulation
Distress Tolerance
Radical Acceptance

~ *What is Mindfulness?* ~

Mindfulness is a way of pausing to avoid
reacting in a foolish way.
It is learning to use both our mind and heart
to make decisions of importance.
Mindfulness involves observing our body
sensations to identify feelings.
With mindfulness we learn to separate fact
from wild assumptions.
At times it is fully participating in what we
are doing in the present moment.
It is freeing oneself of judgments that fuel
anger, resentment, and hurt.
Mindfulness is doing one thing at a time
and focusing on just it.
When mindful we let go of proving we're
right so we can do what works.
To acquire mindfulness we need to practice
in various ways.
Simply meditating as we breathe in and out
is a way to practice.
Walking slowly with awareness of our five
senses is another.
Learning to do everyday chores with our
full attention is one more.
In a way mindfulness is how we take
charge of our thoughts,
So our wandering mind no longer takes us
where we do not wish to go.

1. Do you often blurt things out that you later regret saying?

2. What percent of your time do you spend thinking about the past, the future, and the present?

3. Do you find yourself being angry when you engage in judging or blaming others?

4. Would it be helpful to you to spend more time focused on your senses instead of your wandering thoughts?

5. How often does your wandering mind take you down the rabbit hole?

REFLECTIONS OF THE AUTHOR

I believe there is real benefit to becoming more mindful, and at the same time there are benefits to doing things automatically. Please strive to spend less time brooding about the past and worrying about the worst thing that could happen in the future. When possible throw yourself into what you are doing.

It is okay to think about your child's fun time playing soccer last night while brushing your teeth the next morning. It is fine to plan a surprise for your spouse while driving to work. Yet there are times to enjoy the present moment while focusing on your driving and the beautiful sunrise.

It is easy with the advance of technology to live life focusing on the TV, computer, iPad, and cell phone. It is not uncommon to see a person stop to see a text on their cell, while they are going back and forth from the TV and iPad screen. I think we can get caught up in escaping our feelings and life by engaging in non-productive busyness.

Mindfulness is a skill we can develop through practice. Meditation and focus on the one thing we are currently doing helps us to be more skilled in this area. In simple terms, mindfulness is about responding mindfully, instead of reacting impulsively. It is about learning to control our mind, so our wandering mind doesn't take us to past painful memories or future worries. I hope my poem is of some help to you in living more mindfully.

1. Write about a time when you were mindless and felt foolish or embarrassed.

_____

_____

_____

_____

2. Write about something you can throw yourself completely into doing and be focused on the present.

_____

_____

_____

_____

3. Write about how your life would be different if you were to stop judging and blaming others and yourself.

_____

_____

_____

_____

§

~ *What is Interpersonal Effectiveness?* ~

Interpersonal effectiveness is learning how to
make and sustain healthy relationships.
It involves objective awareness of our feelings
and the feelings of others.
We cannot be effective if we are too emotional
or if we are blind to all feelings.
Effectiveness grows by taming our judgments,
criticisms, and defensiveness.
It requires the ability to respond mindfully,
instead of reacting out of control.
Skilled communication avoids both passivity
and lashing out.
When we choose to be passive we teach
people to take advantage.
Reacting with hostility and aggressiveness
quickly pushes people away.
In learning to be effective, we must respect
the other person and one's self.
Being a skilled listener who validates others
is most important.
Learning to state our concern without blame
reduces defensiveness.
Speaking honestly about our feelings and
owning our emotions is helpful.
Skillfully asserting our request clearly is
needed if we are to be heard.
Pointing out the benefits of granting our
request is key to effectiveness.

QUESTIONS TO PONDER

1. Think of someone you like to be around. What does that person do that makes you want to be around him or her?

2. Do you tend to react defensively or respond mindfully when you have differences with another?

3. What makes a person a good listener?

4. What does it mean to validate another person?

5. Are you assertive when you need to make a request to another?

REFLECTIONS OF THE AUTHOR

When I was working my second job as a psychologist, I experienced some conflict with co-workers. Although I wanted to place the blame for the conflict on them, it was difficult to avoid realizing my perceptions and poor communication skills were a major part of the problem.

After being confronted by a co-worker, I enrolled in a college class on assertive communication. It proved to be of tremendous help to me both personally and professionally. It helped me to take responsibility for my thoughts, feelings and actions. It also gave me an effective model to use to stand up for myself in a responsible manner.

In facilitating DBT groups as a therapist, I really enjoyed the Interpersonal Effectiveness module. It was fun to role play how being passive, aggressive, and assertive differ. It was also helpful for participants to have a chance to practice assertive techniques in the safety of a group before implementing them in the real world.

My poem hits on many of the key ideas taught in interpersonal effectiveness. I would encourage you to learn the model for effectively making a request. The last four sentences of the poem describe what you need to do to be more effective in getting your wants and needs met.

1. Write about what difficulties you have in effectively communicating with others.

   _____

   _____

   _____

   _____

2. What might be a first step to take to improve your relationship with someone that matters to you?

   _____

   _____

   _____

3. Write about qualities you possess that would make you a good friend.

   _____

   _____

   _____

§

~ *What is Emotional Regulation?* ~

Emotional regulation involves awareness and
the ability to respond wisely.
It's hard but not impossible to learn mindful
responding when compromised.
Our biology and life experience of trauma
can disrupt regulation.
Chronic pain and experiencing frequent abuse
robs us of stability.
Remember an emotion is a physiological
response to a prompting event.
Taking slow and deep breaths, exercise, and
meditation each reduce stress.
Practicing good self-care may reduce our
vulnerability to loss of control.
Identifying and replacing our worry thoughts
and self-blame is essential.
Learning to stop our spoken and unspoken
judgments fosters compassion.
Being assertive may free us of low self-worth
and feelings of resentment.
It is important to practice new and effective
ways of responding.
With proper skills and practice we can move
from victimhood to empowerment.
In doing this we will experience a sense of
control and peace of mind,
And reap the benefits of living our life
with emotional stability.

1. What triggers you to have a melt down?

2. Who do you worry about in your life who has difficulty managing their emotions and reactions?

3. Have you noticed that when you neglect taking care of your physical needs that you're more irritable and likely to overreact?

4. Do you talk to yourself as a friend, or do you engage in critical and blaming self-talk?

5. What has over the years helped you the most to better manage your emotions?

REFLECTIONS OF THE AUTHOR

It is quite apparent that we are not all created equal, and we each have grown up in our own unique environment. As a therapist I have encountered so many who have experienced various types of childhood abuse that have impacted both their mental and physical health. They have endured painful events never experienced by those who have lived in more loving and safe families.

Post-traumatic stress disorder (PTSD) affects persons in ways it is difficult to understand. Some live in an almost constant state of high anxiety and hyper-vigilance. I believe that there are therapies that can be profoundly helpful to many who suffer the effects of PTSD. I also know that there are some who on their own have resolved their trauma and experience what is called post-traumatic growth.

If you find yourself struggling with issues of emotional instability, I encourage you to seek the help you need. In my poem there are many helpful things you can also do on your own. Practice mindfulness and do things to calm your physiology. Exercise, mindful breathing, and meditation are often helpful. Identify and replace your negative judgments and self-blame with more compassionate self-talk. Surround yourself with positive people who will encourage you instead of being critical. Open yourself to learn new ideas and skills that will empower you and bring you peace of mind.

1. Write about an area in your life where you have difficulty controlling your emotions.

_____

_____

_____

2. Write down important things you do routinely to help you maintain good mental health.

_____

_____

_____

3. Write about one thing you have learned to do that has helped you avoid flying off the handle.

_____

_____

_____

§

~ *What is Distress Tolerance?* ~

Distress tolerance is coping with life's difficulties
without making things worse.
It is accepting that there will be ups and downs
and that is part of being human.
When difficulties arise we have a choice in
how we respond.
Without skills we are likely to viciously attack
or hide like a turtle in its shell.
Rage unleashed can harm others we love
and bring unwanted consequences.
Anger turned inward may result in self-harm
or other self-destructive behavior.
Distress tolerance skills make it possible to
handle challenges differently.
Stopping momentarily to think and take a
deep breath is helpful.
Calming one's physiology by intense exercise
or taking a cold shower is wise.
Using imagery to visit our safe place may
ease our feelings of anxiety.
Talking with a supportive friend or doing an
act of kindness may bring peace.
Soothing our bodies with a massage and
fragrant smells is relaxing.
When distressed there are countless ways
to ease our tension
In a way that neither causes harm to others
or to oneself.

QUESTIONS TO PONDER

1. What are a few sources of distress in your life?

2. Do you believe you have a choice in how you respond when you are distressed?

3. What happens when you stuff your feelings and don't express your emotions?

4. When stressed, what are healthy ways you can soothe yourself?

5. When you experience intense emotions, what helps you to calm down without engaging in hurtful or harmful behavior?

REFLECTIONS OF THE AUTHOR

There are times that we need to use distress tolerance skills to ease our tension and avoid doing hurtful or unhealthy things. Many times it would be better for a person to take a walk to calm down before discussing a disagreement one has. It is quite difficult to talk rationally when we become intensely emotional.

Many distress tolerance skills are ways to distract oneself from ruminating about a problem or engaging in hurtful behavior. As a therapist, I understand that there are times when we need to experience an emotion or face a problem instead of avoiding it. If you have a strong urge to self-harm or turn to drugs or alcohol to escape your emotional pain, then using distress tolerance skills prove useful.

If you continually avoid facing your problem, you will never resolve it and it will continue to haunt you. It is important to know when to distract and when it is better to face your issues. Talking with a supportive and knowledgeable friend or therapist may help you decide when to distract and when to face your problem.

I hope my poem will help you to accept that distress is a natural feeling and part of life. May it prompt you to think about ways to lessen intense feelings, and the need to at times face your feelings.

1. Write briefly about things that tend to distress you the most.

_____

_____

_____

_____

2. Write about skills you've learned and used to help you better manage distress.

_____

_____

_____

_____

3. Write about how you would like to ideally handle times when you become distressed.

_____

_____

_____

_____

§

~ *What is Radical Acceptance?* ~

Radical acceptance is the willingness to accept
reality — it is what it is.
It does us no good to live in the dream of it's not,
it shouldn't be, or why can't it be.
If it is cloudy and raining, it does no good to think
it should be sunny.
No matter how much we want or try, we cannot
change a single moment in the past.
Embracing acceptance grounds us in the present
and gives us strength to move on.
Fighting reality binds us in chains of frustration,
anger, and self-imposed suffering.
Acceptance does not require us to like or agree
that what happened is good.
Life becomes bearable when we acknowledge
we can't change the past.
It does not prevent us from acting in a way to
improve the situation at hand.
We often get caught up in trying to force others
to change when we need to change.
Do not become lost in past painful memories or
in worries about the future.
Radical acceptance does leave room for hope
and gratitude in hard times.
In almost any situation there is something for
which we can feel thankful.
Accepting reality empowers us to handle life
better and let go of regret.

1. Do you have difficulty accepting reality and frequently think things should be different?

2. What is something that is really difficult for you to accept?

3. How does failure to accept things that have happened cause persons to experience more suffering?

4. What does the following line of the poem mean?
    "If it is cloudy and raining, it does no good to think it should be sunny."

5. Do you find yourself trying to change others and experience frustration as a result?

REFLECTIONS OF THE AUTHOR

Radical acceptance is a difficult skill to acquire, but it often has a positive effect on a person's life. It simply is about accepting things to be the way they are. It does not stop us from taking constructive action to improve things, but it does prevent us from wasting countless hours worrying about the future or regretting things that have happened in the past.

The poem points out that it is futile to live in the dream of it's not, it shouldn't be, or why can't it be. Judging something to be bad or blaming others or oneself does not solve problems. Owning our problem is often the first step in beginning to solve it.

The radical acceptance poem also reminds us that we are quick to blame and believe others should change, when we actually need to change something we believe or do. In almost any situation we can find something to be thankful for if we look hard enough.

Take a moment now to think about how accepting reality helps us to handle life better and empowers us. Make an effort to be more accepting of what is and strive to be less blaming of others and yourself. In doing this you will experience less frustration and find more peace.

1. Write about something that happened in your life that you found was really hard to accept.

    _____

    _____

    _____

    _____

2. If you eventually were able to accept it, what steps did you take to get there?

    _____

    _____

    _____

    _____

3. Write about someone you know that is suffering because they have not accepted something that happened.

    _____

    _____

    _____

    _____

§

SPIRITUAL POEMS

As a therapist and author, I value spirituality and know that faith and hope are often a part of emotional healing. I respect the diversity of persons' beliefs, and I also understand that some persons have unfortunately experienced manipulation and shaming in the name of religion.

The five poems in this section of the book are Christian-based and speak of a loving God. I do not believe that you necessarily need to be Christian or even believe in God to find meaning in them.

~ Allowing Another to Care ~

It is often easier in life to help someone else
than accept help from another.
When someone offers to lend a caring hand
it's easy to say, "You needn't bother."
But in a way we are depriving that person
of an opportunity to share,
Because our ego is too big to allow another
to show us care.
Life is filled with many lessons of learning
to give and receive.
If we're only willing to give, then we're missing
an important part of life I believe.
Did not our loving Lord teach Peter to accept
the Master washing his feet,
And did our Lord not ask the Apostles to pray
with him in his time of need?
If you require a caring hand it would be wise
to open your heart,
And allow the other person to do an act of
kindness on their part.
By accepting the care of another willing
to share and freely give,
You will be opening a door that will lead
to a better way to live.

QUESTIONS TO PONDER

1. Are you too proud at times to allow others to help you?

2. Do you find it easier to help others or to accept help?

3. How do you feel when you do something to help a family member, a friend, or a stranger?

4. How do you think others feel when you accept their help and show genuine appreciation?

5. Have you learned something from this poem?

REFLECTIONS OF THE AUTHOR

I use the "Allowing Another to Care" poem with Christian clients who are having difficulty accepting help from others. When I was a child, my father would give you his shirt off his back if you were in need, but he would not accept charity from others.

I remember him fuming with anger when he had stopped to help someone who had broken down on Route 66 on his way home. He had driven the person to an auto part store and then back to their car. The man offered Dad five dollars and he refused. When he arrived home, he found that the man had stuck a five-dollar bill in the seat. Although he was furious, he would have done the same thing.

If you tend to be too proud to allow others to help you, then rethink what you're doing. Are you not depriving others of the good feelings they would have if you would graciously accept their assistance? Would your life not go better if you allowed others to lend you a helping hand?

1. Write about a time when you went out of your way to help someone in need. How did you feel?

_____

_____

_____

2. Write about a time when someone went out of their way to help you. How did you feel?

_____

_____

_____

3. Write about some steps you might take to become more open to allowing others to help you.

_____

_____

_____

§

~ *The Healer of Broken Hearts* ~

There are times when dusk comes,
And we fear the sun will never rise.
At those times our hearts are broken
Beneath the weight of despair and grief.
Through faith and love we know
He will heal our broken hearts.

There are many questions for which
No answers at this time can be found.
And yet our minds search on and on
In confusion and futility as to why.
Through faith and love we know
He will heal our broken hearts.

We may never understand the extent
Of emotional pain one can endure.
Without fail the tender heart breaks
More easily than the hardened one.
Through faith and love we know
He will heal our broken hearts.

At times of blinding darkness
In emptiness we turn to one another.
We discover He is present in our love,
And we open our hearts to Him.
Through faith and love we know
He will heal our broken hearts.

We share our thoughts and fears,
We share our feelings and tears.
He is present within our hearts,
And his spirit strengthens our lives.
Through faith and love we know
He will heal our broken hearts.

Again and again through parables told,
He reveals God's mercy to us.
His love is greater than
We can ever possibly know.
Through faith and love we know
He will heal our broken hearts.

One so dear has left us
For this moment in time.
But love has no boundaries,
And in time we will be reunited.
Through faith and love we know
He will heal our broken hearts.

Although it may be the darkest of nights,
The Son has risen to light the way.
We will together share the burden,
And his Spirit will see us through.
Through faith and love we know
He will heal our broken hearts.

He is the Healer of broken hearts,
And for this we are surely grateful.
Through his grace in times of grief,
No shattered heart is beyond healing.
Through faith and love we know
He will heal our broken hearts.

1. How does the loss of a loved one affect you?

2. Does your belief system bring you comfort and hope?

3. When you lose someone dear, do you get caught in an endless search as to why one dies?

4. Do you believe there is a God? Do you believe in a life after death?

5. What brings you comfort when you lose someone you deeply love or care about?

REFLECTIONS OF THE AUTHOR

I wrote "The Healer of Broken Hearts" to lend some support to my sister and her family after my niece took her life. As a therapist, I know that suicide occurs much more frequently than homicides, and seldom does it make headline news unless it is a celebrity or there is a homicide involved.

Suicides often happen because the person involved is experiencing deep emotional pain, has lost hope of things improving, and is burdened with negative and irrational beliefs that simply aren't true. I hope that someday there will be more effective treatments for those experiencing a deep depression with suicidal urges and feelings of worthlessness.

I feel this poem is more appropriate for persons of the Christian faith who are struggling with the death of a loved one who died much sooner than one would expect. I hope it will lend hope and comfort to persons who are grieving.

1. Write about the loss of a loved one. How did you handle the news, the funeral if you attended, and being around others who were also grieving?

_____

_____

_____

_____

2. What do you think the author intended in the following phrase? "Without fail the tender heart breaks more easily than the hardened one."

_____

_____

_____

_____

3. Write about what actions you took that helped you heal from your loss.

_____

_____

_____

_____

§

~ *Thank You for Today* ~

Thank you loving Lord for today,
And help me do your will in some way.
Open my eyes to see those in need,
So I may do a kind and simple deed.

Let me appreciate the wind and sky,
As I walk and see birds quickly fly.
Let me bring laughter and a smile
To friends I happily visit for a while.

Plant a seed of hope in my heart,
And help it grow as I do my part.
Each day possibilities are open to me
To become who you want me to be.

Keep me grounded in humility,
As I soar in love that sets me free.
Remind me to be quick to forgive,
So I may enjoy the peace you give.

May I have compassion for others,
And give care to my sisters and brothers.
I am most grateful for my health,
And the life you give is my wealth.

Help me to trust in your love,
And appreciate grace from above.
Again I thank you Lord for today,
As your love shows me the way.

1. Do you experience happiness as you practice gratitude for the many gifts you experience?

2. Are you appreciative of the beauty of nature, or do you find yourself lost in the world of technology?

3. Do you value the freedom to choose?

4. Are you quick to forgive, or do you find yourself frequently brooding about things you believe to be unfair that happened to you in the past?

5. Are you grateful to God, to the universe, or some higher power for today?

REFLECTIONS OF THE AUTHOR

I believe gratitude contributes to our happiness, and I frequently encourage my clients to practice gratitude in some way. Positive psychology experiments have shown that over the course of three to four weeks writing three new things each day that a person is thankful to experience can increase one's happiness. It trains the mind to look for the positive, instead of focusing only on the negative.

"Thank You for Today" is a poem and a prayer of thanksgiving. I do value compassion, kindness, and love. In this simple poem I highlight a few of the things I am thankful to experience. I love to be outside on a nice day, so I can take in the beauty of nature. There are so many wonderful sights, sounds, smells, and sensations of touch we can appreciate when we are open to nature.

I hope my poem touches you in some way. Experiment with gratitude and notice any changes in feelings that you have when you show genuine gratitude. How might your life be different if you were to show gratitude for each and every day?

1. How do you usually feel when you have thoughts of gratitude?

I feel absolutely Marvelouse and at peace.

2. What part of the "Thank You for Today" poem did you most like?

3. Write about several things that you are most grateful to have or experience.

§

~ *Lord, Help Me Forgive* ~

Although I have been wronged
by another,
I have chosen to do more harm
to myself.
The rage and anger I hold within
my heart
Is like venom poisoning the body
until there is no life.
Lord free me of this poison so
that I may have life,
And let peace of mind and happiness
live within my soul.
Help me to stop my self-destructive
judgment of another,
As I accept your will, forgive me as
I forgive others.

1. How does holding a grudge affect you?

2. Do you agree that holding onto rage and hate poisons your emotional life?

3. Do you feel hate or anger toward anyone at this time?

4. Do you believe that God or your higher power wants you to have a forgiving heart?

5. What do you believe are the benefits of forgiveness?

REFLECTIONS OF THE AUTHOR

As a therapist, I am well aware of how deep hurt and anger from past abuse can be unleashed on innocent persons. Individuals who have encountered horrific abuse do not want to go through life like a ticking time bomb of exploding anger. Yet many do impulsively go off on loved ones or innocent bystanders, and then feel intense guilt and shame.

Forgiveness can be helpful to many of those persons. I explain that forgiveness is something we do for ourselves. It is letting go of the internal poison of ruminating thoughts and hate that robs the individual of peace of mind and happiness.

I encourage persons to take the steps that are needed to move forward in life. I feel that my poem on forgiving may give them just a little more understanding of why it is helpful to forgive. If you are stuck in angry and vindictive thinking, I hope you will let go to make more room in your heart to experience peace and love.

1. Write about an event in your life where you feel you were unjustly wronged.

_____

_____

_____

2. Have you fantasized getting back at the person who hurt you? How have you wanted to get even?

_____

_____

_____

3. Write about your experience of forgiving someone.

_____

_____

_____

§

~ *The Path of Grace* ~

One night I dreamed that my entire life
was symbolized by a path.
As I stood in the present and gazed back,
I saw many hills and valleys.
As my eyes followed the path, I could
actually trace it to my birthplace.
The valleys reminded me of the hurt and
feelings of shame from the past.

As I stood in the present and looked ahead,
I saw the future symbolized.
I experienced a feeling of apprehension and
panic as my eyes followed the path.
It twisted and turned up a mountain until
it ended at a grave bearing my name.
In my dream I cried out to God, and I heard
his voice ask, "What is your concern?"

"Dear Lord, as I looked to my past I did not
once see you along the path.
Where were you when life was difficult and
I needed your hand?"
My Lord replied, "My name is I Am. It is
not I was.
You will suffer much if you live in the past,
because I am not there."

"Lord, as I looked to my future I again could
not see you once upon my path.
I greatly fear having to travel to my death
without you being there for me."
I heard the voice of the Lord reply,
"My name is I Am. It is not I will be.
You will suffer much if you worry about the
future because I am not there."

I turned to my side to view the present and
my Lord was standing beside me.
He extended his hand in love and I
reached out to Him.
His eyes penetrated my soul melting away
my hurt and fear.
At last I understood the meaning of
God's holy name.

1. What percent of your waking hours do you spend thinking about the past?

2. What percent of your waking hours do you spend worrying or thinking about the future?

3. What percent of your waking hours do you spend being focused on the present moment?

4. What might you do to stop brooding about things that happened in the past?

5. What might you do to stop worrying about what could possibly go wrong in the future?

REFLECTIONS OF THE AUTHOR

My daughter's favorite poem is "Footprints in the Sand". It served as inspiration for me to write "The Path of Grace". Of all the poems I've written, this is my favorite one. It captures the meaning of mindfulness, and it is about letting go of past painful memories and future worries. I have given it out to many clients over the years.

When Moses conversed with God appearing as a burning bush in the Old Testament, God commanded Moses to return to Egypt and to meet with the Pharaoh to free the Israelites from Egyptian rule. Moses asked God who he should say sent him when he met with the Pharaoh. God's reply was to say that he was sent by, "I Am that I Am."

In therapy, I tell clients to never follow the words "I am" with anything they don't want to be. How often do people make comments like, "I'm so stupid," "I am a terrible mom," or "I'm impossible to live with." I believe the words "I am" are powerful and encourage clients to say things they want to be. "I'm intelligent and wise," "I am a loving mom," "I'm a caring person" and "I'm easy to love" are examples of what type of things we would benefit from saying that follow "I am."

1. Write about a worry you have about the future that at times interferes with your peace of mind.

_____

_____

_____

_____

2. Write about a past regret or painful memory that robs you of happiness in the present.

_____

_____

_____

_____

3. When do you feel closest to God or feel a sense of real purpose in your life?

_____

_____

_____

_____

§

I hope you will find poems 26 to 30 to be helpful to you in your DBT practice. I have tried to summarize important information from each of the four modules of DBT into the five poems. I divided the Distress Tolerance module into two poems titled, "What is Distress Tolerance?" and "What is Radical Acceptance?"

If you facilitate a DBT Skills Group, I would suggest that you use the poems as a mindfulness activity. For example, when beginning the mindfulness module, have the group read the "What is Mindfulness?" Then have them select either one of the questions to ponder or one of the Journal to Heal prompts to reflect on. Have participants express what they experienced and their reflection.
The five poems are:
"What is Mindfulness?"
"What is Interpersonal Effectiveness?"
"What is Emotional Regulation?"
"What is Distress Tolerance?"
"What is Radical Acceptance?"

In doing individual DBT therapy, you may give a copy of any of the above poems to encourage your client to reflect on that aspect of DBT. Poems can assist clients in grasping new concepts and reinforce the use of DBT skills. I hope these poems will prove helpful in your practice.

REFERENCES

Achor, Shawn, *The Happiness Advantage,* (New York, Crown Business, 2010)

Daily, Steve, MS, *Secrets of Psychological Strength,* (Kansas City, Self-published, 2017)

Hahn, Thich Nhat, *The Miracle of Mindfulness,* (Boston, Beacon Press, 1975)

Jampolsky, Gerald G., MD, *Love Is Letting Go of Fear,* 3rd. Edition, (New York, Celestial Arts, 2011)

Koerner, Kelly, *Doing Dialectical Therapy,* (New York, Guilford Press, 2012)

Linehan, Marsha M., Ph.D., *DBT Skills Training Manual,* 2nd. Edition, (New York, Guildford Press, 2015)

Peck, M. Scott, M.D., *The Road Less Traveled,* (New York, Simon & Schuster, 1978)

Seligman, Martin, *Authentic Happiness,* (New York, Free Press, 2002)

ABOUT THE AUTHOR

Steve Daily is a psychologist with over thirty-five years of experience. He is currently in private practice at Northland Behavioral Health and Wellness in Gladstone, Missouri. He is also an author who writes books to bring inspiration, emotional healing and empowerment to his readers.

Steve started his career as a psychologist at Nevada Sate School and Hospital working with adults with mental retardation. When the Nevada Satellite Clinic opened, he transferred there and worked primarily with children with developmental disabilities. His third and final job with the Missouri Department of Mental Health was working five years at Woodson Children's Psychiatric Hospital in St. Joseph, Missouri. There he did psychological evaluations and individual and group therapy with adolescents.

In 1988 Steve took a job as an adult and children's therapist at Tri-County Community Mental Health Center that was located at North Kansas City Hospital. When outpatient mental health services were dropped at the hospital, he went into private practice. He worked in several locations including the Northland Behavioral Health and Associates in North Kansas City and the Kansas City Psychiatric Group. He has spent his last ten years at Northland Behavioral Health and Wellness in Gladstone.

Visit the author online at FeelGoodEnough.com.

CPSIA information can be obtained
at www.ICGtesting.com
Printed in the USA
LVHW091839100223
739049LV00001B/39